HOLDING ON TO YOUR KIDS:
Essential Keys To Effective Parenting

Table of contents

Chapter 1

The importance of parents

There are no terrible kids, simply awful guardians". The significance of Parents in one's day-to-day existence is very apparent from this prominent citation. Being a parent is a capable endeavor and there's no discussion on that subject.

In this speedy time, it is very challenging for guardians to check their presence in their youngsters' life.

Millennial youngsters who are presented with versatilities of interruptions find it challenging to track down an association with the normal. Also, kids are very dazed by the rule of the virtual world.

Significance of Parents in Life

Kid advancement lies its root in their folks. Nothing can defeat the inflexibility of a kid's childhood. A parent subsequently goes about as a visionary to their kids. A few significant focus that discussion about the significance of guardians in youngster development towards training is referenced in the underneath Downloadable PDF.

Guardians and kids strolling inseparably Guardians assume a significant part in their kids' life. They are the mainstays of help, direction, and love. Family is where life starts and love goes on forever. Regardless of how old a kid arrives' nothing is more consoling and mitigating than their parent's arms.

The job of guardians in a youngster's life is past provoking.

Nurturing makes a move sometime before a youngster's introduction to the world and at last guardians become their kids' change inner self as well as the other way around. There is no one like them who can shape and form a kid's way of behaving and improvement.

So guardians ought to never seize to motivate and help their kids and consequently guardians ought to endeavor to be the best educator in their youngster's life.

Keeping a decent Parent-Child relationship is the most vital move towards shrewd nurturing. Right from the introduction of their posterity, guardians ought to know about the colossal dependability and responsibility in their youngster's life.

Cheerful family with father, mother and two children

Concentrates on show that an embryo's personality improvement is capitulated by the changes in its mom's considerations during pregnancy. Not giving the legitimate direction and love can truly influence a youngster's life and can have serious effects that will prompt person deserts.

The parent is the youngster's most memorable educator and will stay a predictable guide in a kid's life.

What is the job of Parents in a Child's life?
To foster abilities
Nurturing is an endless expertise. When you sign for it there's no thinking back. You should assume responsibility and capitalize on your time. Nurturing and kid improvement are in a cooperative relationship.

At the point when one twists, the other consequently tracks down balance. What's more, this is the fundamental rule of each and every parent-kid relationship.

Guardians taking their child for cycling

Guardians add to the mental, socio-social, physical, mental, and profound improvement of a person. Parental qualities and skill assume a fundamental part in the sound childhood of a youngster in this multitude of regions.

The groundwork, everything being equal, The profile of mental capacities, convictions, moral qualities, adapting protections, and striking profound temperaments that describe every kid at each formative stage is the consequence of different impacts working in complex ways.

Most understudies of human advancement concur that the main determinants of the various profiles incorporate the acquired physiologic examples that are called sensitive characteristics, parental practices and character, nature of schools joined in, associations with peers, the ordinal situation in the family, and, at long last, the authentic period in which late youth and early immaturity are spent.

Petition meeting by guardians

As youngsters create from newborn children to teenagers to grown-ups, they go through a progression of formative stages that are critical to all parts of their personhood including physical, scholarly, close to home, and social.

Backing and direction

The legitimate job of the parent is to give consolation, backing, and admittance to exercises that empower the youngster to dominate key formative assignments. A youngster's learning and socialization are most impacted by their family since the family is the kid's essential gathering. Blissful guardians bring up cheerful youngsters.

Youngster improvement lies its root in their folks. Nothing can conquer the inflexibility of a youngster's childhood. A parent in this manner goes about as a visionary to their kids.

mother helping her kid out in schoolworks

There's nothing common that comes near the penances of life as a parent. How guardians help their youngsters out of affection will continuously have a permanent comment on the kid's life.

A youngster who has never quit getting a reasonable childhood will keep on progressing until the end of their lives.

Guardians likewise assume a significant part in the self-assurance of their youngsters. To expand the fearlessness of your youngster, read 6 Simple Tips to Build Self-Esteem and Confidence your Child.

Giving a decent way of life
Schooling is one of the milestones in a youngster's turn of events. A well-rounded schooling will give up a remunerating profession to the individual and consequently they can serve society and return its bounties.

mother playing with her children

It is basic to realize how guardians impact the existences of their posterity and assumes a significant part in the kid's physical, mental, monetary, close to home, and vocation advancement.

How might Parents become effective in their jobs?
The significance of guardians is something that youngsters ought to fathom automatically. Not something can be advanced as a moral or moral inquiry.

Concentrates on show that separated from before times, contemporary guardians have a higher opportunity of inability to keep a decent connection with their youngsters in spite of the family unit arrangements that we have nowadays.

This is the way you can fabricate a fruitful compatibility with your kid.

Parent kid communication

Correspondence is the key
Be it any relationship, correspondence is the establishment. Converse with your kid about points other than school and review. This aides in adding to better servitude between the two players.

Participate in exercises with them

You unavoidably invested quality energy with your friends and family. For this situation, accomplish something with your child that is invigorating for them. This will ultimately assist them with cleaning their inclinations.

Apologize when you mess up
Straightforward and authenticity can do ponders in your relationship. Discard your inner self and apologize for your missteps. With the goal that the youngster can bear

upping for themselves during future undertakings.

How could guardians' activities impact their kids?
A new report shows that guardians who effectively communicate with youngsters assist them with creating urgent mental abilities, fundamental abilities, and ultimately flourish to find success. Guardians add to creating concentration, fixation, and restraint in their kids.

They additionally work on decisive reasoning, sympathy, point of view, making associations, and imparting. With a strong parent, a youngster never laments facing challenges and this readies an independent kid. Guardians' collaborations colossally affect the kid's turn of events, be it physical or mental.

Aside from hereditary legacy, youngsters tend to copy their folks in practically any field. This builds the risk of a parent to be a good example for their youngsters. The endeavors from a parent's side incredibly affect their kids.

Guardians with their child on an ocean side.

Despite the fact that every youngster is unique and exceptional in their abilities, guardians are the ones who can shape and help their kids come what may. It is the obligation of guardians to guarantee a no problem at all climate for their youngsters.

"The mentality that you have as a parent is what your children will gain from, more than everything you say to them. They recollect what you are"; these words by Jim Henson caution us about the job of Parents in a kid's life and legitimizes the effect and impact of guardians in a kid's life.

Nurturing is now and again about tracking down satisfaction in penances. What's more, these penances won't seize to delight you over the long haul. A kid with a momentous childhood won't ever neglect to do right by their folks. Guardians are dependable to give the vital food, apparel, safe house, and clinical consideration to the extent that they are capable.

Enlivened picture of father-girl

They are similarly answerable for giving sound schooling and sound information on their religion as well as the ethical preparation of their kids. Similarly, kids are dependable to see the value in their parent's promising endeavors to guarantee a decent life for them.

Having said every one of these, being a parent isn't just about penance, it is likewise helping your kid to dominate their life all alone.

They ought to give up responsibilities regarding their kids so they master critical thinking abilities quite early on. This will lessen the possibilities being left out when they hit adulthood.

Guardians assume a significant part in their youngsters' lives and every one of their activities will exclusively rely on the nurturing methods embraced by their folks. Our future is our youngsters and to guarantee a superior tomorrow, we need to prepare and shape our kids with care and love.

Father-child couple playing with blocks

So every parent should decipher their youngster's characteristics and help them in their general turn of events and in this manner adding to a superior tomorrow. At the point when a youngster is blissful, then, at that point, guardians are cheerful. Guardians do practically everything to make their kid taught and very much regarded in the public arena.

Anything the circumstance or whatever is the issue that a kid faces throughout everyday life, guardians ought to attempt to persuade and rouse them by their own guides to make an intense into great. Guardians attempt to make the equilibrium in their youngsters personal perseverance that assists with advancing predicaments quicker.

Chapter 2

Being a compassionate parent

At the point when tests are not far off, nervousness proliferates. Unease is overwhelming, among kids, however more so among hyper-pushed guardians. Frequently guardians bring their youngsters for directing or treatment just before the tests with only one solicitation - "Fix my kid so he can score great imprints".

A few guardians are so fixated on causing their youngsters to do well in tests that they seem like experts attempting to get their machines to perform at their ideal limit. It concerns me to imagine that these grade-frenzied mothers and fathers are raising the up-and-coming age of residents.

My desire for a superior world pushes me to compose this article on caring nurturing, where each tip I propose starts with a letter in "Sympathetic". Peruse on to find out about how you can turn into a kinder, more settled parent as opposed to attempting to extract out that additional imprint from your powerless, drained kid.

Make a place of refuge: As a parent, your essential obligation is to make a safe profound space where your youngster can impart unreservedly and straightforwardly. Start by welcoming your kid to talk about his thoughts. What's more, when he opens up, tune in! Try not to hinder or reprimand, however, listen non-critically.

Situate yourself in the real world: It is not difficult to get snatched up by the fantasy of your kid besting the tests. Parental strain to perform well scholastically is one reason for India having probably the most incredibly upsetting insights connected with youth and adolescent suicides. Keep in mind, that tests will continue to occur. In this way, don't cause your youngster to feel like a dormant machine intended to produce stamps and top grades constantly. Give her the space she wants, and permit her to perform at her speed.

Propel, yet don't push: You can continuously persuade and move your kid to pursue scholarly achievement, however, there is a scarce difference that isolates positive inspiration from being domineering. Know about when you may be going too far and beginning to push him past his inherent capacities.

Focus on: Even assuming that your kid is showing up for the board test, keep things in context. Tests are not the apocalypse and results are not the most important thing in the world of presence. Have your needs set up. Your youngster's physical and close-to-home prosperity is more significant than scoring almost 100% on the test. Along these lines, deal with her and address her issues.

Stay away from put-downs: For some explanation, guardians believe that put-downs and reactions are successful inspirations for a kid to send off himself into execution mode. Running against the norm can make irreversible harm to your youngster's confidence, making his presentation dive.

Quit looking at: There is no such thing as a sure examination. At the point when you contrast your kid with another, you are giving her the message that she isn't adequate. This is adverse to her mental and close-to-home well-being.

Quit taking out your disappointments on your youngster: Your kid might be worried, yet he may not show it. Assuming you accept that he is simply abiding by his time, you could wind up treating him with mocking. You may likewise wind up dislodging your resentment from different circumstances on your weak kid. Every one of these can break his soul. His exhibition will experience more if you start chastening or mishandling him each time you are disappointed.
Infuse a portion of tomfoolery.

Tests shouldn't turn into the justification behind life becoming dismal! Get some downtime for relaxation and fun exercises, both for you and for your kid. She wants to comprehend that there is something else to live besides tests and that it is OK to require some 'me-investment' out to unwind and sustain herself before walking on with the review.

Notice your kid for indications of stress: Don't turn out to be so centered around the ultimate objective of accomplishing excellent grades that you neglect to see indications of stress or despondency in your kid. Assuming his craving or rest designs have changed, if you notice him becoming calmer and removed, assuming he is more bad-tempered than previously - urge him to discuss his sentiments. If he doesn't, look for proficient assistance before it is past the point of no return.

Support your kid well: As a parent, you should feed your kid's body, psyche, and soul. Give nutritious food, energize day-to-day actual work, and demand adequate rest to guarantee that she stays true and sincerely sound. Imparting values like saying a request and family eating times can be hugely useful in giving the construction, routine, and soundness each youngster needs for solid in general turn of events.

Acknowledge your kid genuinely: I have met my reasonable part of guardians who tell their kids, "I will cherish you provided that you perform well." Such contingent love thus called acknowledgment can in some cases hurt more the kid's mind than even clear maltreatment. Each kid looks for acknowledgment, particularly from her essential parental figures. She wants to hear that she will be adored, regardless of anything. Work on imparting the conviction that you will continuously show up for your kid, no matter what her imprints or scholastic grades.

Show concentrate on abilities: I have seen guardians wear themselves out attempting to 'educate' their kids. My idea to such guardians is to show their youngsters successful review abilities all things being equal. Permit your kid to make his schedule; you don't do it for him. Allow him to get a sense of ownership with his presentation, not you. Allow his imprints to be his own, not yours!

Engage your kid to confront difficulties: Your youngster needs to comprehend that achievement and disappointment are a piece of life. Bombing a test ought not to be depicted as a disaster. Rather, guarantee your youngster that she can compensate for it in the following test. Above all, you want to mean it when you let your kid know that it is OK to come up short. Keep in mind, that a youngster who never encounters disappointment could never foster abilities expected to adapt to one. Disappointment trains a kid to attempt once more and fabricates his personality. Youngsters who fizzle and drive forward are the ones who grow up to be stronger and effective, and positively more satisfied.

This is what merciful nurturing resembles. You can help your kids feel and deliver their difficult recollections, as well. Here are a few ideas:

Try not to respond protectively, wince, or excuse their aggravation.
Sit with your youngsters and permit them to feel their feelings and express them.
Permit yourself to feel your kids' difficult feelings, as well.
Tell your kids you sympathize with their aggravation, hear them, and see them.
Tell your kids you know the previous hurt them, and you're heartbroken.
Tell your youngsters you won't ever disgrace them for communicating their sentiments.
Tell your youngsters communicating agonizing sentiments about their past is alright.
Pay attention to your youngsters with everything that is in you.Offer them your all-out consideration, backing, and love

Chapter 3

Listening to your kids

Is it true that you are truly paying attention to your children? Furthermore, would they say they are paying attention to you?

They say: "I was simply holding these cigarettes for a companion." You say: "YOU

ARE GROUNDED FOR LIFE. DON'T YOU KNOW THAT SMOKING WILL KILL YOU!"

You say: "Don't take drugs. Try not to drink liquor. Try not to smoke." Your youngster hears: blahblahblahblah

Is it conceivable to stay away from these steady questions and detaches with your children? Most certainly, specialists tell WebMD. You totally can talk so your children will endlessly tune in so your children will talk.

Yet, how would you decipher the code of youth - - without turning to "Haha," "BRB," "TTYL," or other maddening - - yet well-known - - kids? This is the very thing that the specialists need to say regarding paying attention to your children and inspiring them to pay attention to you.

Listen intently.

First and foremost, paying attention to your children makes them bound to stand by listening to you, specialists tell WebMD.

"The main method for talking so your kid will listen is to pay attention to your kid," says New York City psychoanalyst Gail Saltz, MD, writer of a few books, including Getting Smart About Your Private Parts. "If they feel listened to as well, they are bound to have the option to tune in and will feel more comprehended, have more trust, and be keener on what you need to say."

Mark Kopta, Ph.D., director and teacher of brain research at the University of Evansville, in Indiana, concurs. "You are significantly more prone to get a kid to pay attention to you on the off chance that first, you pay attention to them," he says. "My brilliant rule is, 'The point at which you experience difficulty with a kid, pay attention to the first and afterward feel for them.'"

How it's done: "The primary thing I would do is stand by listening to the kid or teen, then, at that point, reflect how you think they are feeling, and afterward move into the main thing in need of attention," he prompts. For instance, if you get a kid with a bunch of cigarettes, get some information about it and pay attention to what he says. Then, urge your kid to discuss his sentiments, and mirror the sentiments back as precisely as possible. Maybe he had a go at smoking since his companions were all making it happen, or because he needed to seem more seasoned - - two strong motivations for naive youngsters and teenagers. He might have the cigarettes for an entire host of reasons, so making a move prematurely is significant not. Whenever you have figured out what is happening, you will be better ready to manage what is happening.

Pay attention to yourself first.

As indicated by the American Academy of Pediatrics (AAP), it is vital to consider what you intend to say before you answer your kid. Guardians frequently offer unforgiving expressions bitterly or disappointment. You may not exactly mean the furious words, but rather your kid might very well always remember them. "Neglectful remarks or jokes that appear to be coincidental to you might be pernicious to your kid," the AAP states. "Phrases like 'You inept simpleton,' 'That is a moronic inquiry,' or 'Don't irritate me' cause your kid to feel useless and undesirable and may genuinely harm his confidence." If you continually censure or put your kid down, he might wonder whether or not to ask you inquiries or pay attention to what you need to say.

Try not to address it.
At the point when you do have the floor, "addressing is not an effective method for

getting your kid to tune in," Saltz says. All things being equal, go for "connecting endlessly talk that asks what they think and cultivates their reasoning cycle and independence," she says. For instance, "Ask your kids, 'What is your take on drugs, liquor, sex, or how the educator dealt with a specific circumstance?' and that way you can start a conversation where there will be compromise and they will likewise be bound to pay attention to your viewpoints," Saltz says.

"Ask teenagers inquiries and let them reach their inferences - -, for example, 'What are the awful things about ingesting medications?' - - rather than saying, 'These are the terrible things about consuming medications,'" Kopta adds. "This all returns to a high schooler's craving for freedom."

Be near - - a great deal.
"Everyone maintains that there should be a decent setting and time to have a significant

talk with their youngsters, however, kids work on their schedule, so the main thing is making an opportunity to be near," Saltz tells WebMD. "You need open doors that don't feel too high-forced, similar to 'now we will have a discussion.'"

Assuming that you are proposing an awkward subject like medications or sex, up close and personal discussions might make things more troublesome. All things considered, have a go at talking in a vehicle where your kid can take a gander at the rear of your head or during a walk when you are side-to-side.

Give your kid space.
At the point when your kid starts responding to you with one-syllable responses, make a stride back, Saltz says. "Ask them what they are feeling, which will ideally assist them with thinking about why they are offering one-syllable responses,"

she says. Then, at that point, say, "I might want to discuss it, however, if you believe you can't right now, we can refocus in several hours or tomorrow."

Move your kid.

"So frequently guardians say 'don't get pregnant, don't get a physically sent sickness, and don't take medications,' and those are three discouraging discussions," brings up Rabbi Shmuley Boteach, a New York-based family and relationship guide and host of The Learning Channel's Sholom in the Home.

"What motivation would any children take from those discussions?," asks Boteach, writer of a few books, remembering the impending Sholom for the Home. "All things being equal, attempt to have motivating discussions that provide youngsters with a feeling of what is significant," says this dad of eight. "At the point when your children get back home, ask them what occurred in school and have a story for them."

Try not to shout.
"Be harsh, yet assuming you holler at kids that shows you are crazy and you establish a non-quiet climate," Boteach says. "There must be a quiet climate at home." Remember, that youngsters flourish in strength. "Converse with your children, give them severe guidelines, make sense of them, and rebuff youngsters when fundamental, yet don't let completely go and holler," he prompts.

Underscore the positive.
Make the up-sides equivalent to the negatives, Kopta says. "Individuals seldom change in light of adverse results, generally nobody would smoke, drink or gorge," he tells WebMD. "It's sufficiently not to tell a

kid not to smoke, drink, or consume medications except if you present elective things to give them positive sentiments - - like games, music, workmanship and relations with others.

.

Chapter 4

Solving problems carefully.

What is Your Decision-Making Style?
There are many styles of deciding, going from extremely normal and straight to natural and unfurling. Take this

internet-based evaluation to decide your style.

Find Your Decision-Making Style

Would you like to improve or clean your style? Consider the numerous rules included beneath.

Rules to Problem Solving and Decision Making (Rational Approach)
A lot of what individuals do is take care of issues and simply decide. Frequently, they are "under significant pressure", pushed, and extremely short of time. Therefore, when they experience another issue or choice they should make, they respond with a choice that appeared to work previously. It's simple with this way to deal with stall out surrounded by taking care of a similar issue again and again. Along these lines, it's frequently valuable to become acclimated to a coordinated way to deal with critical thinking and independent direction.

Not all issues can be addressed and choices made by the accompanying, rather levelheaded methodology. Notwithstanding, the accompanying fundamental rules will kick you off. Try not to be scared by the length of the rundown of rules. After you've rehearsed them a couple of times, they'll turn out to be natural to you — enough that you can develop and improve them to suit your requirements and nature.

(Note that it very well may be more your inclination to see an "issue" as an "opportunity". In this manner, you could substitute "issue" for "opportunity" in the accompanying rules.)

1. Characterize the issue
This is frequently where individuals battle. They respond to what they think the issue is. All things being equal, try to see more about why you believe there's an issue.

Characterize the issue: (with input from yourself as well as other people). Ask yourself as well as other people, the accompanying inquiries:

What might you at any point see that makes you believe there's an issue?

Where is it working out?

How is it working out?

When is it working out?

With whom is it working out? (Here's a clue: Don't leap to "Who is causing the issue?" When we're worried, accusing is much of the time one of our most memorable responses. To be a powerful chief, you want to resolve gives more than individuals.)

For what reason is it working out?

Record a five-sentence depiction of the issue as far as "The accompanying ought to occur, yet isn't ... " or "coming up next is going on and ought to be: ... " As much as could be expected, be explicit in your portrayal, including what's going on, where, how, with whom, and why. (It could be useful as of now to utilize an assortment of exploration strategies.)

Characterizing complex issues:

Assuming the issue appears to be overpowering, separate it by rehashing stages 1-7 until you have depictions of a few related issues.

Confirming comprehension you might interpret the issues:

It assists an incredible arrangement with confirming your concern investigation for meeting with a friend or another person.

Focus on the issues:

On the off chance that you find that you are taking a gander at a few related issues, focus on which ones you ought to address first.

Note the distinction between "significant" and "dire" issues. Frequently, what we view as significant issues to consider are simply critical issues. Significant issues merit more consideration. For instance, if you're not kidding about "earnest" calls, you've most likely got a more "significant" issue and that is to plan a framework that screens and focuses on your calls.

Grasp your part in the issue:

Your part in the issue can extraordinarily impact how you see the job of others. For instance, assuming you're exceptionally worried, it'll presumably appear as though others are, as well, or, you might resort excessively fast to accusing and denouncing others. Or then again, if you feel exceptionally remorseful about your part in the issue, you might disregard the accountabilities of others.

2. See possible foundations for the issue

It's astonishing the amount you have hardly any insight into what you don't have any idea about. Hence, in this stage, it's basic to get input from others who notice the issue and who are affected by it.

It's frequently valuable to gather input from others in turn (basically right away). In any case, individuals will generally be restrained about offering their impressions of the genuine reasons for issues.

Record your viewpoints and what you've heard from others.

Concerning what you think may be execution issues related to a representative, it's frequently helpful to look for counsel from a friend or your boss to confirm your impression of the issue.

Record a portrayal of the reason for the issue and as far as what's going on, where, when, how, with whom, and why.

3. Recognize options for ways to deal with resolve the issue

Right now, it's valuable to keep others included (except if you're confronting an individual or potentially representative exhibition issue). Conceptualize answers for the issue. Conceptualizing is gathering whatever number of thoughts as could reasonably be expected, then screening them to track down the smartest thought. It's basic while gathering the plans to not condemn the thoughts — simply record them as you hear them. (A magnificent arrangement of abilities used to recognize the basic reason for issues is Systems Thinking.)

4. Select a way to deal with resolve the issue
While choosing the best methodology, consider:
Which approach is probably going to take care of the issue as long as possible?
Which approach is the most practical to achieve for the time being? Do you have the assets? Is it true or not that they are

reasonable? Do you have sufficient opportunity to carry out the methodology?

What is the degree of chance related to every other option?

(The idea of this step, specifically, in the critical thinking process is the reason critical thinking and navigation are profoundly coordinated.)

5. Plan the execution of the best other option (this is your activity plan)

Cautiously consider "What will what is going on resemble when the issue is addressed?"

What steps ought to be taken to execute the best option in contrast to tackling the issue?

What frameworks or cycles ought to be changed in your association, for instance, another strategy or technique? Try not to fall back on arrangements where somebody is "about to put in more effort".

How might you be aware on the off chance that the means are being followed or not? (these are your signs of the progress of your arrangement)

What assets will you want concerning individuals, cash, and offices?

How long will you want to carry out the arrangement? Compose a timetable that incorporates the beginning and stop times, and when you hope to see specific marks of progress.

Who will essentially be answerable for guaranteeing the execution of the arrangement?

Record the responses to the above questions and consider this as your activity plan.

Convey the arrangement to the people who will be engaged with executing it and, in any event, to your nearby manager.

(A significant part of this move toward the critical thinking process is constant perception and input.)

6. Screen execution of the arrangement
Screen the marks of progress:

Is it true or not that you are seeing what you could anticipate from the markers?

Will the arrangement be finished by the plan?

If the arrangement isn't being followed true to form, then, at that point, consider: Was the arrangement reasonable? Are there adequate assets to achieve the arrangement on time? Should the greater need be put on different parts of the arrangement? Should the arrangement be changed?

7. Check if the issue has been settled or not

One of the most outstanding ways of confirming if an issue has been settled or not is to continue typical tasks in the association. In any case, you ought to consider:

What changes ought to be made to stay away from this sort of issue from now on? Think about changes to approaches and strategies, preparing, and so on.

In conclusion, consider "What did you gain from this critical thinking?" Consider new information, understanding, and additionally abilities.

Consider composing a concise notice that features the outcome of the critical thinking exertion, and what you realized thus. Share it with your boss, companions, and subordinates.

Judicious Versus Organic Approach to Problem Solving

Judicious

An individual with this inclination frequently favors utilizing a thorough and sensible methodology like the rules in the above segment. For instance, the reasonable methodology, depicted underneath, is many times utilized while tending to enormous, complex matters in essential preparation.

Characterize the issue.

Analyze all likely reasons for the issue.

Recognize all choices to determine the issue.

Cautiously select another option.

Foster a methodical execution intends to carry out the best other option.

Cautiously screen the execution of the arrangement.

Check if the issue has been settled or not.

A significant benefit of this approach is that it gives areas of strength for a request in a generally turbulent circumstance and gives a typical casing of reference from which individuals can convey in the circumstance. A significant disservice of this approach is that it can require a long investment to wrap up. Certain individuals could contend that the world is excessively tumultuous for the objective way to deal with be helpful.

Natural

Certain individuals affirm that the elements of associations and individuals are not anywhere close to so robotic as to be improved by taking care of an endless flow of issues. Frequently, the nature of an association or life comes from how one handles being "out and about" itself, as opposed to the "showing up at the objective." The quality comes from the continuous course of endeavoring, instead of from having fixed a ton of issues. For some individuals, it is a way to deal with hierarchical counseling. The accompanying statement is much of the time utilized while making sense of the natural (or all-encompassing) way to deal with critical thinking.

"Every one of the best and most significant issues in life is on a very basic level insoluble ... They can never be settled, yet just grown out of. This "growing out of" demonstrates on additional examination to require another degree of awareness. Some higher or more extensive interest showed up not too far off and through this widening of viewpoint, the insoluble lost its direness. It was not tackled coherently in its terms, but rather blurred when defied with a new and more grounded life encourage."

Chapter 5

Disarming your Anger

Outrage is a characteristic of human inclination.

Overseeing outrage in good ways sets a genuine model for kids and assists them with having a solid sense of reassurance and security.

Outrage the board strategies can assist you with quieting yourself when you're irate.

If you're finding it hard to control outrage, conversing with a well-being expert can help.

On this page:

Outrage and guardians: what you want to be aware

Why do guardians feel furious once in a while

Perceiving indications of outrage

Straightforward resentment of the executive's thoughts

Setting a decent outrage the executives model for youngsters

Outrage and guardians: what you want to be aware

Outrage is a characteristic of human inclination.

At times outrage can be something to be thankful for. For instance, outrage could give you the energy to finish something or to support what you put stock in.

Feeling irate and dealing with your resentment in good and sound ways can likewise allow you the opportunity to set a genuine model for your kids. For instance, when you take a couple of full breaths or leave instead of detonating, you tell your kids the best way to act.

Yet, outrage can be negative, particularly if it happens a great deal or it gains out of influence. Blowing your top when you're furious can aggravate issues and lead to a struggle with others. At the point when you don't allow yourself to quiet down, you could say or do pointless or harmful things.

Likewise, youngsters need to have a real sense of reassurance and get to develop and grow, so being around a ton of contention and hollering isn't great for them.

Why do guardians feel irate now and then
Bringing up youngsters is a major and significant work. It frequently includes adjusting various requests including work, family time, family errands, youngsters' exercises, and social exercises. At the point when you're in this present circumstance, it's not difficult to become annoyed and feel irate when things don't go to design.

In some cases you could feel irate or baffled with your accomplice, assuming you have one when you disagree on choices about bringing up kids, discipline, and family tasks. Such conflicts can prompt clash, particularly assuming you're feeling sabotaged or unsupported.

Now and again your kid's resentment or dissatisfaction can drive you to feel crazy. For instance, if your kid is furious and talks discourteously to you or will not do as you ask, you could feel yourself flying off the handle as well. You could wind up going after back at the time and thinking twice about it later.

Also, different variables can drive you bound to feel crazy - like disease, stress at work, monetary troubles, absence of rest, and insufficient time for yourself.

It could assist you with realizing that many guardians have explored difficulties like these with the assistance of family, companions, and well-being experts.

On the off chance that you're finding it hard to control yourself when you're furious, conversing with a well-being expert can truly help. You could begin by seeing your GP, who can assist you with making indignation the board plan. Assuming you're furious to the point that you believe you could hurt your kid or your accomplice, leave the room and look for help right away. Call Lifeline on 131 114, the National Sexual Assault, Domestic Family Violence

Counseling Service on 1800RESPECT (1800 737 732), MensLine Australia on 1300 789 978, or a nurturing helpline.

Perceiving indications of outrage
Your body offers you early hints of outrage. At the point when you can perceive these signs, you can likewise do whatever it may take to stop your annoyance from gaining out of influence.

Early indications of outrage include:

quicker pulse
beating stomach
unsettling - that is, feeling tense or surly
quicker relaxing
facial flushing
straining shoulders
grasping jaw and hands

perspiring.

Negative reasoning

Negative reasoning is exceptionally normal when you're furious, and it can aggravate your annoyance.

For instance, you could have had a hard day at work and feel worried. At the point when you get your kids from school, they begin contending in the rearward sitting arrangement, which causes you to feel baffled and focused. When you return home, they will not take out their lunch boxes and set their sacks aside so you feel furious as well as baffled.

Here are a few negative considerations that you could have in this present circumstance:

'Nobody at any point helps me - I need to do everything myself.'

'You kids are so shrewd.'

'Assuming you acted better, I wouldn't feel so furious.'

'For what reason would you like to disturb me?'

If you notice contemplations like these, it's an indication that you want to pause and effectively quiet down before you blow your top and detonate with outrage.

Never shake a child. Infants and children have extremely frail neck muscles to help their enormous, weighty heads. Shaking a child - or hitting, kicking, or tossing a child - can bring about death, inability, or serious injury.

Basic annoyance with the board thoughts
Stage 1: recognize your outrage
The initial step to dealing with your displeasure is to see the early signs. It's truly critical to be aware and say that you're irate, regardless of whether it's simply to yourself. For instance, 'This is causing me furious' or 'I can feel myself blowing up here.

Stage 2: attempt to quiet down
When you notice the early indications of outrage, you can do a couple of things to begin quieting down.

Here are far to quiet yourself at the time, particularly if you can't step away from your kid:

Attempt to slow your relaxation. Take in for two seconds and inhale out for four seconds. Do this a couple of times until your pulse dials back.
If your kid is by and large exceptionally boisterous, have a go at impeding your ears or putting on commotion-dropping earphones briefly. Then take a couple of profound, slow breaths.
If you can remove time from your kid, here are a few plans to attempt:

Accomplish something that calms you, such as paying attention to some music, flicking through a magazine, or simply peering through the window.

Go outside for a run or walk.

Wash up.

Converse with a companion about how you're feeling.

Ensure your kid is in a protected spot before removing time. You could request that somebody watch your kid while you head off to some place calm for a couple of moments.

Signs that you're quieting down incorporate your pulse dialing back and your muscles unwinding.

Stage 3: think about the circumstance

Assuming you feel you've quieted down, it very well may be great to ponder what has simply occurred. This can assist you with gaining experience and handling comparative circumstances better from here on out. Ask yourself:

'How significant is this? For what reason would I say I was so unglued about it?'
'How would I like to figure out this present circumstance?'
'Do I have to take care of this, or might I at any point let it go?'
It's really smart to tell your youngsters or your accomplice how you're feeling and what you're doing about it. It shows them a superior method for dealing with their resentment as well. For instance, 'I'm feeling irate. I want to go outside briefly to quiet down before we discuss this.

Setting decent displeasure the executives model for youngsters
It's OK to feel furious - it's simply not OK to shout or damage somebody.

Assuming you express upset for lashing out, it sends the message that outrage isn't OK. So it's smarter to express upset by shouting or blowing your top. This sends the message to your kids that it's OK to feel irate in some cases however finding solid approaches to dealing with anger is more significant.

What to do when you don't oversee outrage well
There'll constantly be times when you don't oversee outrage well and you holler or make statements you lament.

At the point when this occurs, it's smart to pause for a minute to resolve what to tell your youngsters or your accomplice. Here are a few thoughts:

'Please accept my apologies for blowing my top. In the future, I'll remove myself to quiet down prior.'
'Please accept my apologies I hollered. Could we at any point discuss what simply occurred?'
'Please accept my apologies. I shouldn't have said that, even though I was furious. I ought to have left and quieted down before we discussed it.'

Taking care of yourself can assist you with feeling more settled and better ready to tackle issues with your kids as well as your accomplice, and loved ones.